Master Class Pay Day®

NEVER BE BROKE AGAIN

TITUS MADUWA

Copyright© 2020 Titus Maduwa founder of Master Class Pay Day®. All rights reserved. No portion of this book may be reproduced mechanically, or by any other means including photocopying without the official permission of the publisher. It is illegal to copy this book, post to a website, or distribute it by any other means without permission from the publisher.

Limits of Liability and Disclaimer of Warranty

The author and publisher shall not liable for your misuse of this material.

This book is strictly for motivation, information and academic purposes.

Warning – Disclaimer

The purpose of this book is to motivate, encourage, educate and entertain. The author and/or publisher shall have neither liability nor responsibility to anyone with respect to any loss or damage caused, or alleged to be created, directly or indirectly by the information contained in this book.

JUDICIAL NOTICE:

The Publisher has strived to be as accurate and complete as possible in the creation of this thin book.

While all attempts have been made to verify information provided in this book; the publisher assumes no responsibility for errors, omissions or contrary interpretation of the subject matter herein. Any perceived slights of specific person, people, or organizations are unintentional.

Readers are cautioned to stick on their own judgment about their personal circumstances to act accordingly.

All Rights reserved ©

ISBN: 9781694283214

DEDICATION

I respectfully dedicate this valuable book to (my beloved spouse) Bridget, for her everlasting support and love.

(my dear children) Lindelani & Uhone, for sufficiently showing me unconditional love.

(my lovely sister) Martha (my humble brothers) Simon and Andries. For by heart being an excellent examples.

(my Clients, Audience, Graduates,

Brilliant Students)

without whom this wouldn't be beneficial.

TABLE OF CONTENTS

	ACKNOWLEDGEMENTS	6
	INTRODUCTION	7
1.	**How a village boy turned this around being broke and struggling**	12
2.	**Month end statement! not what. but how?**	20
3.	**Yep, this actually works 5 tips on budgeting**	26
	Budgeting guarantees you take care of the significant stuff	
4.	**Frankly I'm a little surprised better budgeting nuggets**	32
	Every day, I advance my economic lives	
5.	**You're about to miss out on budgeting tools that works**	39
	My expenditure patterns can be controlled	
6.	**Money budgeting software I promise it's worth it**	45
	My bank account can not substitute for the pleasure, passion, and peace that I would save on my life	
7.	**I have good news and bad news**	52

8.		Let's fix your priorities to family budgeting together	58
9.		Read my best 7 steps Master Class Pay Day® family budgeting	64
10.		Why 1000's of my clients are using this smart secrets to budgeting	68
		Start using this new secrets of keeping to the family budget	
		Here's the real reason why you can budget like Mom	
		Bridget (My Wife) surprised me with 10 tips to avoid shopping shortages	
		Do not save your money without this	
11.		BONUS! #.Wallet files; To people who want to create wealth but can't get started	89
		About The Author	124
		Conclusion	125

ACKNOWLEDGMENTS

Master Class Pay Day® NEVER BE BROKE AGAIN. This book is intended to assist others to help themselves. I am eternally excited to all who have graduated from the program and hope some of this sincere gratitude can be repaid by the passing on of their experiences to make a difference to your life.

Master Class Pay Day® NEVER BE BROKE AGAIN book may have been impossible without modeling path walkers who have already crossed the bridge, who have provided me with a vehicle to realize a dream. To name just a few; T.Harv Eker, Robert Kiyosaki, Less Brown, Brian Tracy, Greg Secker, Tony Robbins, Robbin Banks, Nick Vujicic, DJ Sbu et al.

Rich Life Club, Millionaire Mind Intensive, Harv Eker International, Success Resources unconditionally sponsored my personal development study and provided me with everlasting food for thought.

Special thanks to our Clients, Relatives, Fans, Rhema Bible Church, Millionaire Pillars™ Team, Millionaire Pillars™ Book Writing Academy, World Class Trading Secrets® graduates for your endless support.

INTRODUCTION

Knowledge from this book you are able to use it in you life immediately True or True? I hope you said "True."

So; today I encourage you to read this book page by page and stay until the end of the last page.

Because I really think you are going to recognize something you may be doing and not doing that preventing you from creating the success that you really want in your life. So; if you have a cellphone out, email open, skype open, or anything else around you that could distract you. Please do yourself a BIG favour and put it away for now. (PLEASE PUT ANY DISTRACTION AWAY)

I am about to share with you the BIGGEST, what is the word, please? BIGGEST Secrets I know that lead to my success. The secrets that took me from a village boy broke life to urban man upper life. The secrets in this book totally changed my own financial life. And has now changed the lives of my clients, as well

NEVER BE BROKE AGAIN

as my student's lives. And here is the thing: And if you read it, learn it, use it, and more importantly own it. I believe it can change your life too.

In my early career, I wanted to be successful as an employee. I was willing to do what it took to be successful. But no matter what I did, no matter what I tried, I ended up broke. Or nearly, not as successful as I wanted to be. I struggled for a very long time. In my very last employer, It was my very last job in a row, that was a burst. I was losing hope and I was totally depressed. One day I met a gentleman, who was over at the house sitting in his car. He was extremely well informed. He stopped and we begin talking. The gentleman asked me if I am interested in reading and I nodded my head with an answer "YES." He borrowed me the book and we agreed on the deadline for me to return the book. The gentleman told me this statement; "Titus, If you're not doing as well as you'd like, all that means is that there's something you don't know." I almost fell off my chair...

Being broke ever-smiling young at that time I thought I knew everything. But obviously, it was not the case. The gentleman was staying in the wealthy urban area next to my place. I respected him. I sucked up my ego for a change and started to listen to the gentleman. He said to me: "You have to realize, that wealthy people generally think and do things, the same way." He begins asking me this question: "Titus what do you want in life? I told him I wanted to help people to solve their problems in their careers or business. The gentleman said something so simple, so obvious and it just shocked me. It boiled down to this; he said: "Titus if you want to impact people in career or business, why don't you study wealthy businesspeople and learn what they do and how they do it?" Huh!

Guess what? After reading that book my expenses were minimal at that time. Actually I devoted the next six months half a year studying wealth people. I actually found many, many, many similarities and principles they seemed to use. And they all had in common. He invited me to go and attend wealth seminar, and I showed up. So it was time to put my newly acquired information to the test. And I didn't have money as you know. Instead of concentrating on the lack of money, I became resourcefulness. What do I mean by that? Reading and going to wealth seminars became my habit. I volunteered to work on one of the largest global event organizations in the world. I absorbed everything in learning, reading and implementing all the strategies. These strategies worked! In fact, they worked so well, and I ended up being promoted from a crew member, reseller and up until I have been appointed as a strategic partner.

To cut the story long short, Currently I am an Amazon published author, the founder of Master Class Pay Day® NEVER BE BROKE AGAIN, Millionaire Pillars™ Book Writing Academy as well as World Class Trading Secrets® program. People, who know me from the past started to ask me how you went from an unhappy life to a life of happiness in a very short period of time? I began sharing and coaching some of the information I have learned. And the information seems to really resonate with them because it was obvious they were making the biggest mistakes that I have made earlier on.

By the way; pretty soon these reasons, principles, tips, strategies were making a huge difference in their lives too. So I began sharing the wisdom with my beloved people. So today in this book I'm going to reveal something, I've never pinpointed before. Here is the thing: Anyone who read this book today and implements all the strategies, tips and principles can go from unfulfilled life to a life of extraordinary in just a few short years. So are you ready to get started with the first chapter? I hope you said "YES." Let's Go.

NEVER BE BROKE AGAIN

1 CHAPTER

How a village boy turned this around being broke and Struggling

> *"Financial peace isn't the acquisition of stuff. It's learning to live on less than you make, so you can give money back and have money to invest. You can't win until you do this."* – Dave Ramsey

Learn how Titus applied Master Class Pay Day® NEVER BE BROKE AGAIN 80/20 Pareto principles in his life & coaching business.

Did you know that there are only four parts to every business to succeed?

Here it's what I have figured; I didn't understand, what's called, "The 80/20 rule. Where basically 80% of your success is determined, by only 20% of your actions. It also applies to save and budgeting as well. Listen closely; there are four major part to every business. Let me explain them: Product or production, Operations or administration, finance which includes budgeting and marketing, which also includes sales. Please, don't get me wrong everything above is important when it comes to getting wealthy.

However; only one of the above elements is simply a lot more important than the others. So now I have grouped all four parts into like that, can you guess which one is more important than the others? I think you know by now; it's marketing.

It is marketing, that will have the single biggest impact on your business and therefore, your entire spending, budgeting as well as your financial life. Why? Simple. Without marketing, you have no clients or customers. Without clients or customers, you have no money to save or spend. If you are a strong marketer, you will make a fortune. If you are a mediocre marketer, chances are, you'll always be broke. Or very close to it. It boiled down to this: I have never met a good marketer who was not financially successful. It took me so many years of struggle to figure this out. And I am not ashamed to mention that I grew up in a remote village of Muumoni in Limpopo South Africa. When I finally did, my life was not the same as I was.

In this book, I am here to give you some of the shortcuts that will help you more faster than my situation before. It will be, your knowledge and expertise in marketing that will determine whether you have massive success and get wealthy or you have a major struggle, and you stay broke and poor.

I am recommending this to you; I want you to focus most of your time on your life, career, business, money, and energy, and learning into the field of marketing and sales. How much? A full 80% of your time, 80% of your money, 80% of your energy, 80% of your learning all that into marketing.

Here is the most important piece of information that I would like to remind you of. Where do you get all your money from? Think about this for a second. In business you get all your money from other people, in nine to five jobs you get all your money from your employer. People are the only element here on earth that uses a currency called "Money" Every Rand, Dollar, Pound, Yen e.t.c have to be given to you by previously mentioned sources. Meaning, that's where you have to put your attention. On them. Not you. On their needs. Not your product. Here is the thing; your product it is important only when it relates to your clients or customers. And if your message doesn't do that, it is dead in the water. Still, in this chapter, I just gave you, one of the Holy Grail, in creating wealth.

It's about them, not about you. If you read this book until the end and have the ability to do that, my friends your life won't be the same. Allow me to say this again; if you read this book until the end and have the ability to do that, my friends your life won't be the same. The challenge is, this is a very rare skill. If it wasn't; everybody in business would be wealthy by now. Most people are now broke and poor at their best and now you know why? The key is not the product. The key is marketing.

NEVER BE BROKE AGAIN

Let me ask you something. How many of you have ever tried to sell something and heard the word, NO? I am betting most of you, right? And how many of you who heard NO! A lot? When I was starting marketing on one of my program called Master Class Pay Day® NEVER BE BROKE AGAIN for the first time. I heard the word NO! Forty times a day. And the word YES only three times a day. I did not give up. By applying the principles, tips, and strategies in this book. I started to hear NO! Five times a day and the word YES! 30 times a day. Now you can do the maths. That's 10X more success. That's 10X more income that I made. And the big difference is that I was an expert in what? Marketing. I have understood the power of the Customer Value Optimization and Marketing Conversion Cycle.

How to put out the right message. To the right people. At the right time. To get them to raise their hand and say, I'm interested. And then, how to convert those interested people, into buyers. These people, they basically continue to buy from you, for the rest of your life! Allow me to introduce these concepts to you. Ready? The headaches in the business are in the front-end. But the money is in the back-end. Let me repeat this so that you can feel it; The headaches in the business are in the front-end. But the money is in the back-end.

The big paycheck is in what you get from your job, while you provide or sell to your customers after, they become a client on an ongoing basis. In our Master Class Pay Day® NEVER BE BROKE AGAIN program we will help you to create a big back-end for your financial life, career, and business. Only if you want to be wealthy. And if you are going to work with me, I hope being wealthy it's your intention because that's my expertise. My target audience is people who are serious about creating wealth for themselves, their families and contribute to others. If you want to be super successful and really wealthy you need to be, a big fish, in a little pond.

NEVER BE BROKE AGAIN

You don't try to be all things to all people. Why? People don't want to buy from what they think are generalists. They want to buy from experts.

If you have an unsupported belief of having a lot of money. Then that's a problem. It boiled down to this: That belief is not serving you, your family and the other people you could actually be assisting. Because again, if you have a lot more money than you need you can help a lot more people, that need it. It is good if you use your money in a good way and all those principles are all covered in this book. Be wealthy, use your wealth, in a positive way.

Why else do people not put enough attention, on the marketing side of their business? And so quite naturally, as human beings, we tend to veer away from things we're not very good at. Let me remind you of these principles: If you want to be wealthy, learn from the wealthy. Here is the one reason why people don't like marketing. They hate to sell. And they equate marketing with, selling.

In reality marketing is selling, however, there is a big difference in format. My friends, everything happens for a reason and I am a big believer in that. Because I was forced to find ways to market or sell or have people buy from me without the risk, of personal rejection. You know what? If you understand that, you can literally write your own ticket in this universe. It is the most valuable knowledge or skills a person can possibly own. And it doesn't work only in business or your finances it also works in a relationship including yourself.

Selling is pretty well, one-dimensional. But marketing is multi, multi, multi-dimensional. Meaning there are hundreds of ways to do that. There are videos,webinars, teleseminar, blogging, direct mail there are so many ways where you never have to speak directly to anyone person. And still, end up with sales and customers.

2 CHAPTER

Month end statement! not what. but how?

> *"Money often costs too much." –
> Ralph Waldo Emerson*

I'm going to get straight to the point here; because I've created something in this book that can literally change the course of your whole life, in just a short period of time!

Yes, you heard it right, in just a short period of time. And what's even better, is that you'll discover the fastest way to implement the below principles and strategies that you've been missing in your life.

That it's generally not what you do. It's how you do it, that makes the biggest difference. It is not what kind of paycheck, it is how do you spend that paycheck. Is it the what of just marketing? Or is it, how you do your marketing? The key is to market in a way, that is not only effective.

But that, yourself resonate with. And that you actually enjoy it! Remember, if you don't market in a way that resonates with who you are, you will fail at it. Allow me to repeat this; if you don't market in a way, in a format, in a style that resonates with who you are and what you actually enjoy you will fail.

Albert Einstein once said..."Energy can neither be created nor destroyed; it can only be changed from one form to another.' And in this case, from one person to another.

Here is the thing: If you and your format, resonate and are one with you; your marketing will be what's called, congruent. It will be solid, it will be strong. My friends here are other secrets. Don't ever use the word; it's a four-letter word "SELL." By the way: What is the reason that someone would even consider buying your product or service? Here is the qualified answer, you are solving, some kind of problem for them.

It boiled down to this; people give you their money because you are solving a problem for them. If you solve a problem for one person, you make money. And if you solve a problem for some people, you make some money. Again if you solve a problem for a lot of people, you make a lot of money.

Starting from today going forward, you are to never use the word "SELL" again to anyone. You have to replace the letter word "SELL" with "HELP." Always come from a simple place of helping other people. Always come from the direction of service. Make a habit of trying to really make a real difference in people's lives in a big way or in a small way.

If you do that, I promise you; you will not only have a lot more meaning and fulfillment in your life. But you are going to be way more financially successful. What I am sharing with you here, it's critically important to your financial success and happiness. Every morning when you wake up, you have to say these words out loud to yourself. "I help people, not sell people."

Some people may say, It is easier said than done. Here is the statement that I would like you to program on your mind; every master was once a disaster."Here is the question that I always ask one of my daughters and her name is"Uhone."

I go asking here like this; "Uhone, can you really expect to be great at something without really focusing on it? Without taking it really seriously? Without putting the time and energy and effort into it? Uhone replied, "NO" Daddy, that one is not possible." Only if Uhone can say that and how about you?

Here is the Holy Grail I am giving it to you; everyone who is a great or even good at something, had to learn how to do it. If you want to keep your money on your payday (I mean end of the month.), learn how the wealthy people use their money wisely.

Remember I am also using some examples here like you learning how to be an effective marketer in your new start-up or existing business and the bottom line is; only if you master these principles you can apply it in your career and as well as your entire life.

These principles works and now I over-deliver these strategies on our Master Class Pay Day® NEVER BE BROKE AGAIN Program, World Class Trading Secrets® Coaching Program, and Millionaire Pillars Book Writing Academy™.

I teach them in a way that is simple, usable and most importantly, it creates real the transformation for people. People buy with emotions, and they justify their decision with, logic. Here is another secret; if you want to be wealthy, not only in money but in heart and fulfillment then you also must give. You also must serve. You also must truly help. Not because you are making money; you really need helping people.

I love children so much and here is another question that I always dazzle with my firstborn daughter. And her name is "Lindelani." And here is the question "Lindelani; what is the use of being wealthy, if you are unhappy and you are not fulfilled? Lindelani replied; "Being wealthy, enhance happiness, and we deserve to work on both."

I am instantly giving you some gold nuggets in this rare book. Do you know how you naturally feel when you give someone a great gift, and they absolutely love it? And they use it all the time. And you typically made them really, really happy.

Well, how do you feel? Great! Right?

NEVER BE BROKE AGAIN

3 CHAPTER

Yep, this actually works 5 tips on budgeting

> "Don't tell me what you value, show me your budget, and I'll tell you what you value." – Joe Biden

If you're really serious about progressively changing your current life to the next level, then this efficiently is the ideal crucial step. Not only does it work, by continuing reading this book it's the tiniest investment you can make and still have a realistic expectation of your end results.

So you could say that it's kind of amazing right?

In fact, after reading this chapter you will realize your commitment to your future starts here:

What is common's a modest budget for? A

budget is a means to manage your finances by managing the family costs in such a manner that cash is sufficient for the payment of bills and ensures funds are still made available for potential spending- holidays or child schooling and even pension.

It's excellent for you to invent your own strategic scheme to maximize money by raising commodity rates day by day, and ensure every penny you earn is adequately invested.

Establish your effort to coordinate your expenditure and list of expenses that may influence how you use your revenue and empower you as an active person on your financial stabilization.

Your revenue source, lifestyle, spending habits, present employment and location, living costs, payments, and credits will determine your budget needs. Starting with your funds remains the best route to succeed in an area of self-fulfillment and achievement.

NEVER BE BROKE AGAIN

The following advice and suggestions will provide you with information on how to aid you to handle your finances and take responsibility for your expenditure from a distinct perspective.

- Treat Math–Allow all the calculations in your buying requirements as your life partner. Try matching rates for a variety of food and family products you need on a daily basis across your present place.

In an object, you are attempting purchasing, save as much as you can. For example, Chinese traders use efficient purchasing methods and you can model them too. You save as far as you are able and generally buy in quantity to save your income CPI on your items.

- Gambling–Start the graph to make your life easier as it could be. Gambling will seize you away from your funds and make you susceptible to bankruptcy risks.

NEVER BE BROKE AGAIN

- Accurately know your wishes and needs –Limit your expenditure on something you don't need. Luxuries are second to casinos in aspects of the degree of money-stripping capacity, according to the latest research.

- "Do not spend more than you earn"– the tales of Rags-To-Riches are not without mentioning this popular cliché. This phrase is always true because you can't reside in a globe where you eat more than you can generate.

- Keeping a roster–It's essential to make your own timetable plan to make your achievement prudent. A clever customer must think about the quantity of a certain commodity and how it will affect his personal lives.

While he or she has money to purchase for you, an unconscious end user wouldn't worry what you buy.

You can not afford to disregard this advice and go ahead with your exercise unless you are someone with a substantial quantity of riches and earnings.

Budgeting guarantees you take care of the significant stuff.

It makes my life simpler to plan ahead. Budgeting is one way to implement schedules. It guarantees the first items that are essential are done.

I have a priority and a discipline in how I use cash. It's important for ongoing success to be mature about my financial approach.

I am stagnant because frivolous expenditure prevents me from investing significant funds in the important stuff. So I remain on track for my economic well-being. I hold my eyes on my objectives.

I concentrate on both my mandatory fees and the items that give me equilibrium when I budget. While it's nice to pay attention to potential plans, mentally and spiritually it's nice to look after myself.

Every month, I undertake to physical fitness for some of my income. I understand my body is my mind and soul's exterior shell, so it merits well-treated.

It's a nice way to relax by booking cash for amusement. If I can set up frequent downtimes in my life, I'm more efficient.

While I like to go with my colleagues to dine and drink, I do so with moderation. Persistent scrimping on these pursuits is a sure way to lose track of goals in adulthood.

Now, the reason why I undertake to budget every month is I have religious, physical and economic health intact. I am confident in my achievement of objectives, as I secure funding to arrange for a successful mission.

4 CHAPTER

Frankly I'm a little surprised better budgeting nuggets

> "Wealth is not his that has it, but his that enjoys it." – Benjamin Franklin

Call me crazy Master Class Pay Day®, but I'm a little surprised you still haven't given up on reading this book.

Why should you read further? If you've got to think high to rise...

Most people are unaware their life follows a trajectory. What do I signify by that?

That is, your level of success and achievement in anything is predetermined! I repeat this word PREDETERMINED! By your psychological state.

Here it's a secret READY? Your state of mind determines how successful you will be in life.

The self-concept in this book is YOU and how you see, feel and interpret yourself in relation to the world around you.

Your Self-image here; it is how you see yourself in relation to the world. Specifically, it is about the images which are playing in your mind and how you interpret them subconsciously.

And your Self-ideal here; it is about the ideals you have and how close you are to achieving them. When you are more tunes with your ideals, you feel good about yourself.

Also your Self-esteem here; it is about your emotions and how you feel on the inside. With good emotions flowing through you, you feel worthy and interpret things more positively.

It boiled down to this...

Primarily, a budget is a cash scheme that outlines your economic objectives.

A plan that allows you to identify and control resources, meet and attain your economic goals, and to decide in advance how your finances work well.

The principal idea in saving or budgeting is to spend a certain amount of money on both anticipated and unexpected costs. Budgeting simply implies an estimate of the monthly household expenditures based on prior expenditure and charges.

The first stage in budgeting is to determine how lengthy your pay will last. Fixed charges such as vehicle fees, house rentals, insurance, etc. You can also carefully track your expenses for one month to find out and comprehend where your money go. You can instantly define alternatives for efficient budgeting by correctly defining your "expenditure habits."

For instance, when you have a steady monthly income of $3,000, in zar R45,000 you should subtract all your identified monthly bills from that income.

You can evaluate other charges and then remove them from your revenue quantity.

Your bill in the family can now be your equilibrium after set expenses.

Instead, economic plans enable you to use ratios or percentages rather than spending cash for various products such as oil, apparel, leisure and food.

The key alternative for effective budgeting is rigidity and efficiency ; set expenditure must be used to make deposit inflexible.

Budgeting will operate better if very limited omissions are produced. The concept here is to formulate objectives and schedules, and then keep to them whenever you can.

Here are some advice on budgeting:

1. Are you great at managing cash. Your behavior is important. Get an arrangement and compromise and understand how important it is to cut costs ; all this includes much effort.

NEVER BE BROKE AGAIN

2. Plan the scenario for you. Make a list with one hand of your income and the other half of your overheads.

3. Know the distinction between need and luxury. List what you think to be luxuries, divide the record into part, cross part of the roster.

4. Nevertheless, practice humility with respect. With little or no expenditure, you can have pleasure at all. Play with the children on the beach or in the mall instead of traveling shopping.

Budgeting is an efficient and basic instrument that everyone can easily access. Consider it and take advantage of it.

Every day, I advance my economic lives.

I understand the significance of and I operate to achieve economic safety. It's worth me to be financially safe. I operate every day to improve the quality and future of my economic lives.

I address them immediately when I see economic difficulties. Something can always be experienced from a struggle. Because of the economic barriers I face, my life is enhanced.

By paying my bills on time, maintaining my borrowing under command and saving for the future, I guarantee a good economic existence. I'm gaining more than I'm spending.

I can also assist others through the improvement of my economic lives. I'm mentally able to help all my relatives, friends and society.

NEVER BE BROKE AGAIN

I can consider acquisitions and create excellent decisions much more easily rather than spending cash upon purchasing impetus, which I may regret subsequently. I am not getting too many charges because of my sparingness. It's essential for me to have sufficient cash.

I can concentrate on my career because I have enough funds. All stuff I appreciate to save, invest and donate to others. I could do this because the money assigned to me I care about. To assist others effectively is very essential to me, and each day I do so easily and gladly.

I'm working to enhance my economic career and progress it today.

5 CHAPTER

You're about to miss out on budgeting tools that Works

> *"You must gain control over your money or the lack of it will forever control you."* – Dave Ramsey

Yep, this is pretty much your opportunity to acquire all the tools that work at Master Class Pay Day® book here. Therefore you better approach it now because chances are you won't read or see it again anywhere for quite some time.

My friend; your blueprint for success this year depends on you being able to set a plan in motion that not only leads you to your financial goals but clearly sets out the individual steps to take as you implement it.

Does that sound like something you need help with? In that case, you're not alone.

NEVER BE BROKE AGAIN

Would you like changing your personal life and financial life forever? If so, have a look at the following chapter that I have brought for you below:

It doesn't have to be incredibly difficult to budget your monthly costs to get the biggest yield on your revenue (And maybe even set some aside to save!).

Diverse budgeting programs can be used. Cash leadership programs offer a common bundle that enables you to access your money flows and outflows, categorize your expenses and sometimes analyze your expenditure.

You can also enter the different transfers you have to create on a monthly basis through these programs, and then monitor if you have earned your duties on a moment. In relation, some projects also offer you a tax form proposal that will help you make sure you don't miss out on any fees or deductibles, for that issue.

NEVER BE BROKE AGAIN

Coupons are an additional budgeting instrument you can use. Multiple shops and journals have coupons that you can use to get discounts on different products. If you need to buy a specific item for which you have a coupon, you'll wind up storing a portion of what you might have had to invest on a periodic buy.

Lists–whether you are on document, mobile device or private electronic secretary (PDA)– assist you concentrate on buying, and maintain record of your transactions. Please note that you need to maintain track. Your periodic food journey is a standard instance.

Plan the full list of the week and define what meals and equipment are not available in your shopping cart before you make the journey. Instead register other family objects you have been missing from (or will eventually end before you can create the next journey to the foodstuff).

You can go to the grocery store armed with these plans and understand precisely where to go and what to purchase. You walk silently along the aisles without such records and probably pick up various food items that you probably won't need in the near future or you have already at work.

One of the finest budgeting devices in your house is perhaps a filing system. You can collect your receipts, checks and any bank records you send when you save or deposit, using a straightforward marked file folder.

You can hold record of how much you charge and when your payments are due by compiling your deposits, loan card accounts and the like.

Appropriate budgeting instruments are the ones that finest meet your consumer needs. Create your own budgeting instrument or discover a program that fits your environment.

My expenditure patterns can be controlled.

Self-control in other parts of my lives needs me to manage my costs wisely.

I predict that days will be difficult than normal when goals fulfill. These days are the drive to keep my expenditure practices under management and I'm making it a point to save for rainy days.

My personality reflects how I invest. I'm frank with myself, so what I can afford is frank. I live an uneasy life so I make sure I don't have to care about placing food on my table because of my expenditure practices. I pledge to invest wisely and efficiently.

Occasionally buying instinct is a real challenge as I feel I need to do what I want to invest. I'm looking at the larger image for a time.

I imagine what the result might be if I create the payment and refrain from purchasing the product if the problem exists.

I pledge today to work tough to keep my expenditure patterns under control. I understand that sometimes there are economic circumstances that change my intentions, but I commit myself to doing them as well as I can.

6 CHAPTER

Money budgeting software I promise it's worth it

> *"Happiness is not in the mere possession of money; it lies in the joy of achievement, in the thrill of creative effort." – Franklin D. Roosevelt*

I recognize your greatness. I see you were put here on the planet to complete a mission.

My friend; I appreciate you have the ability to step fully into that mission. I equally perceive what you're tolerating. You're tolerating a sense of unease.

Waking up, already feeling frenzied and overwhelmed. Feeling slightly disappointed every time you don't perform all the things you stated you were going to do.

Not going on vacation or taking time off because; you don't have either the money or the ability with all of your responsibilities. I know it's extremely frustrating.

And the hardest part is; you may have forgotten to a point where all of those tolerations see "normally" now.

And you don't know how to shift it. Right?

Here's what you need to know, my friend. All those tolerations come from two places.

1. Not having a clear idea of the steps, you need to be taking in your personal, financial life or business.

2. Not knowing how to plan those steps out in a structured way that allows you to get them done.

Because planning is actually a form of self-care. It frees you to take the pressure off yourself and actually hit your financial goals again and again with less work than you're doing now.

As promised and it's worth it. I want you to read the budgeting software planning steps below:

Nevertheless, several people argue that they cannot just budget by themselves. You ensure requiring some help to develop a sound and viable budget.

It seems some economic experts have created some money budgeting software that will make it easier to set up a good budget to promote smart money-saving methods.

The issue for most individuals nowadays is that through loan cards, they get so happy with their costs. They indulge in cashless buying that ever more individuals spend more than they can buy.

Experts therefore argue that budgeting can certainly ease the "economic burden" of customers by administering expenditure and revenue rather than dropping into the pot of debts.

It seems some economic specialists have developed software for cash budgeting that will allow for the development of a healthy plan to encourage sensible strategies to save cash.

In essence, cash money management software helps a person to spend and utilizes the cash sensibly. These fresh techniques assist to divide cash into different dimensions and regions and contribute to investments.

There is a list of its advantages if you don't understand still what the software for the cash budgeting can do for you:

1. It enables you to monitor your cost. You can certainly hold track of your expenditures with the money budgeting tools. You can comprehend your cash stream with this kind of technique and you can know how much money you invest and gain.

2. Although some individuals are relaxed with the normal form of paper-based budgeting, using a money-budgeting tool can offer you more than you would imagine. You can even produce certain predictions using the embedded tools for cash budgeting. You can even sign them for record maintaining if you are truly in hard copies.

3. The issue for the most individuals who do not have a plan is that they usually spend more than what they have. It provides you power.

You can monitor your expenditure with this type of assistance. If you're already spending too much or not, you can understand. Moreover, you are attentive to the blast of all your cash decisions.

The upper row is that software for cash budgeting can definitely guarantee and regulate the kind of certainty you need to monitor your costs.

NEVER BE BROKE AGAIN

This enables you to be more sure than simply indulgent, that all your actions are focused on purpose and schedule.

My bank account can not substitute for the pleasure and passion.

I'm glad I've got cash and I can use it to take care of my family. However, the funds itself will never fulfill my requirements. My loved ones fulfill my deepest requirements.

I value my cash and I understand how to make intelligent use of it. I'm using it to support life's bigger stuff. Life's finest things are not things; families are the finest things in life. I'm not in a cash bond.

I don't praise or hate cash. Monetary funds are just a resource. My life is a series of pleasure and my pleasure highly infectious. I can bring pleasure from different sources with my favorable approach.

When I see the rays of sunlight gleaming through the wolves, I am happy to watch kids practice and laude.

Passion is an essential element in my career. I'm lovely and I understand I've been deeply cherished. The greatest donation I have got is love and devotion. Knowing that my mistakes are forgiven and that I am loved, despite them, is sincere satisfaction.

I am conscious of my blessings by concentrating on my existence. There are several experiences that have great effects on my life, and I use images and publications to conserve my experiences. I've got a lovely career!

Whether my bank account is complete or void does not matter. I belong to love, joy, and gladness. I understand what my true treasure is whether I earn the universe or loose it all.

7 CHAPTER

I have good news and bad news

> *"Money is a terrible master but an excellent servant."* – P.T. Barnum

If I were to speak straight to your heart, I'd ask you, Do you want me to start with bad or good news? Which one will you prefer?

By the way; enormous success comes not merely from having a radical plan for your life but also from knowing how to put that plan into action, step by step.

If you are someone who's income is dependent, then this is an opportunity you cannot miss!

If you're tired of the struggle as well as worry, and stress of living month to month paycheck and client to client in your business, you need to follow the below techniques.

NEVER BE BROKE AGAIN

By reading and taking action, it will put you in a position to make strides in your finance, personal, business that most people and entrepreneurs only achieve after years and years of trial and error.

As regards to economic safety, the urgent funds are regarded to be necessary as they can provide you with the economic assets to which you can rely on and rely upon if a crisis occurs so as to pay tremendous medical charges or unexploited house or significant vehicle repairs if you are ill.

The Bad News

If one does not have an urgent budget, you can borrow several years to pay back the debt from your credit card, which would be so much more expensively.

The Good News

But by placing an additional $30-$50 a month in zar R500 on a separate "urgent money card," you can ensure that in the future will deliver some returns.

It is advisable to regard the Emergency Fund as a supplementary payment, which should be charged on time every month.

Indeed, the additional cash for an urgent loan can and must be made available and allocated, since it is extremely important to refer to its' economic potential.' In this respect, you aim to save money on your revenue, which should usually be equivalent to your working expenditure for at least three months.

What is essential is to keep a certain quantity of cash and use it only in actual situations.

The achievement of our long-term pension fund, not like an undertaking, does not really depend on the quantity of profit or interest, but on the continuous and constant removal of a set quantity of cash to provide instant entry.

As can be seen, by your economic position, you know where your cash is actually eaten or used for the final phase in the phase of building an urgent loan.

If one acknowledges and determines where one's income are being invested, then it will be simple for one to choose and decide where to cut spending, that is, saving.

Budgeting is putting or setting aside money for anticipated and unanticipated future use. It is here that one sets up a goal so as to save. So set an emergency fund as your goal.

The spending plan provides for the projected and unintended use of cash or allocates it. Here, you set an objective to save. Set your financial goal on an urgent budget.

Either your investment objective, urgent money, or both can be achieved. You can use the cash raised by adding part of it to the bank and quarter for requests in your savings account. Thus, you attain your investment objectives while also providing urgent funding. This is your decision.

NEVER BE BROKE AGAIN

Staying in my ways guarantees my household economic liberty.

Since I have a powerful feeling of self-discipline, I can support my family. I'm greater than my appeal to material belongings to be safe from economic stress.

I'm disposing of associations that make me combine my merits with my tangible belongings. Whichever thing I may or can not handle, I am looking for mates who enjoy me and value me for what I am.

I withstand the desire to get stuff for others to please. I stop purchasing products just to demonstrate off from my cost spectrum. Even when I'm out with buddies, I always remain inside my expenditure.

I am convinced enough that I do not buy out of personal duty. When I go out with my friends, I feel fine and I'm the only one who can't buy an object or choose not to buy something.

I know that life occurs in cycles, and I can handle more in the future. I choose to be grateful in everything I have at this stage.

I understand it does not ensure pleasure to have more stuff. Real pleasure emerges from a core that is grateful.

The most important thing for me when I shop is how my acquisition can impact my family, not how it can impact the view of others about me. In keeping with our expenditure, whatever the circumstances, I respect my family.

Currently, to set things up for financial stability, I choose to cast off ego. I happily create small changes today so that my household can appreciate a stronger future.

NEVER BE BROKE AGAIN

CHAPTER 8

Let's fix your priorities to family budgeting together

> "A wise person should have money in their head, but not in their heart." – Jonathan Swift

This is one of my preferred times of the year because; I get to spend time with my family and celebrate all of the amazing things I am grateful for.

I look forward to finishing this year knowing I have plans in place to make next year a brilliant year with you.

- Will you be part of the VIP winning audiences? YES! :)

- Will you be joining me for a climb to the top of Mt.Kilimanjaro with the devine Master Class Pay Day® Tour Experience? INDEED! :)

- Will you be present at my workshop as a VIP guest audience? DEFINITELY! :)

Good Job! My dear friend!

Sometimes occasions might cause the dispute in the household bill. The main employee takes the ultimate economic choice most of the time, which is not always a pleasant agreement. As cash remains such an essential component of household lives, parents must come to an agreement in this area. The budget for household cash is a four-step process for peace and harmony.

1. Set goals for you.

Different experiences from objectives. You, as a family, want to concentrate on, say safety or the future of children, are elements of your household lives. When outcomes are particular targets supporting priorities.

Do not put too many goals as it fails the objective. Ideally, there can be only one, but two to three are sensible because existence is not perfect.

NEVER BE BROKE AGAIN

Write them down as the goals are established and decided. Publish the document where they can be seen by everyone to remind them of the focus of your community for the next few years.

2. Name your objectives.

When objectives have been established and decided by the household, the next phase is to establish financial goals. Objectives are particular and measurable requirements that will help the goals when they are attained.

Establish a goal in achieving objectives that is both difficult and achievable. A healthy investment goal for a child's potential schooling is 10-15% of his revenue in the Family: spraying, yet attainable.

Try to regulate your household on establishing one to two objectives per concern, to stay focused.

NEVER BE BROKE AGAIN

3. Strive to achieve your objectives.

Start staying with it after you have set your objectives. All the activities of the family are designed to achieve your goals. Follow the advancement of revenue and expenditure tracking tools, in particular with regard to economic objectives.

The easiest route is to have a notebook and record all costs and revenue and create a timetable for potential expenditure. There are those who spend on computer software or an accountant for a household. Whatever it is, the significant thing is to have a family quality surveillance scheme in order to achieve their objectives.

4. Examine the lives of your household.

When it's a moment for you to assess your lives, verify how your household works against the goal at some stage. The objectives that have been accomplished can be verified off the roster and fresh designs can be developed.

Sometimes, in major changes, it may be time to re-evaluate goals, tell a professional change, or when a household mate leaves. If a moment like this arrives, the process starts, just like what it is for existence!

I'm glad to give.

It's a joy to give to others because it reminds me I'm happy. To be willing to offer, I count it as a privilege. I am blessed every day and look forward to bonding with others.

I'm the one who gains when I lend to others. After getting my donation, seeing the look of happiness on someone's face makes everything worthwhile. My donation emerges from the core, so even when I feel blank I keep providing.

With no cords tied, I voluntarily offer. I am abstaining from contest, contrast, and boasting because I am giving on the basis of what I can offer, whatever others may offer.

I'm safe from stress, I chose to offer. I've spent a ton of moment and thought about my offering. Before I present a donation, I am packed with happiness and enthusiasm for the recipient's response.

It's more enjoyable to give than to receive. It's invaluable to know that I've helped a individual in their need. Just as in my moment of need I would like others to be there for me, I'm there for others.

My donation is not only monetary or material; I also offer of myself.

I create it a point to be active in the time when I am around my loved ones and to pay all my attention to them. I work for worthy causes because it makes a distinction to give my time and power.

Now, by opening my arms lovingly, I have a choice to influence the lives of those around me. The more I offer away, the more I'm gaining!

9 CHAPTER

Read my best 7 steps Master Class Pay Day® family budgeting

> *"An investment in knowledge pays the best interest. – Benjamin Franklin*

Imagine that you had a very wealthy friend or mentor sitting down with you for approximately 60 minutes and reveal his biggest, most impactful financial life lessons that took him from being broke to really, really rich.

Would you listen?

If you're committed to learning, growing and becoming successful, then YES, of proper course, you would. If so, accomplish whatever you can to implement the entire 7 steps in this chapter below.

NEVER BE BROKE AGAIN

This remarkable chapter is precisely an absolutely a game-changer if you're carefully looking to upgrade your personal life, financial and business.

It is about time to overhaul the possible way people look at budgeting. It can actually be a great way to keep track of your family's expenditures and help you evaluate the things that you spend the lion's share of the family's earnings on.

Some people habitually think of a plan as a fog. It is painful to see how difficult it is to make a deficit and to realize that you can effectively destroy the whole item with one incorrect buy. And for most breadwinners, this has been typically a constant nightmare.

Start these easy measures to prepare a household plan without worry, and see the advantages of smart expenditure.

1. Collect your salary receipts for three months and earn your monthly average income.

2. Have your additional fees out for three months. Use it for the monthly specified charges such as lease, telephone bill, vehicle bills and other credits. Fill in and get the median. Include other costs, such as food and credit card charges.

3. Assess your calculations ' outcomes. Take a glance at your monthly average earnings compared to your monthly set costs and other monthly expenditures. Reduce certain objects which are pointless somehow.

4. Revealing the truth about your revenue and expenditures, developing a household plan and trying to keep up with this monthly plan.

5. Set up a bank plan now that you have a monthly deficit. Save up by making regular deposits to this account.

6. Keep track of this monthly family budget just to see if it is working for you. Seek to fine-tune the "rough spots" of this spending plan as you go along.

NEVER BE BROKE AGAIN

7. Only when you can use personal financial planning software or chart to keep track of your budget, the better. It makes it pretty easy to organize your costs.

It's these fundamental measures to formulate a monthly household budget, which is easy to adhere to. Naturally, every family needs and wants various things. You have the freedom to develop your own monthly family budget, depending on your family's financial background and needs. No matter what you do, concentrate on the end result, which creates savings that will give your family a bright and financially stable future.

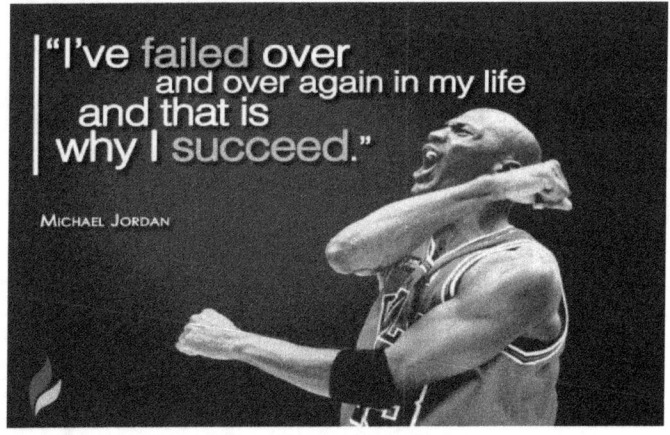

NEVER BE BROKE AGAIN

10 CHAPTER

Why 1000's of my clients are using this smart secrets to budgeting

> "Learning is the beginning of wealth. Learning is the beginning of health. Learning is the beginning of spirituality. Searching and learning is where the miracle process all begins." – Jim Rohn

How much is it worth to you to know you can develop successful financial habits which will automatically carry you into a happier and more prosperous life?

Can you really put a price on that?

When it really comes down to it, this isn't about "rands, pounds, dollars, and cents" This is about financial control, empowerment, freedom, and security.

NEVER BE BROKE AGAIN

Here's an official statement I get a lot, something to this effect and I will give you some free of my coachings below before we jump into smart secrets of budgeting. Ready?

Someone will say. " I want to get out of debt and create a passive income so I can put 100% of my focus on my passions and interests. I have lots of things in my life that I want to do and accomplish."

Do you know what the problem is here? I call it "means-to-an-end" living.

Here is the thing my friend:

You can focus on your passions or interests, and the other things you want to do in your life without being fully financially free and fulfilled. If you wait to be rich before you do this, you might wait for your whole life. You'll be too old to do them by then.

Don't wait. Do it NOW! You don't have to be perfectly, financially free to do what you love to do.

Do it in the way you can enjoy it right now. If there's a secret to balancing your personal life, that's it you make time to follow your passions, three days a week, two to three hours a day.

It's not going being perfect, but most people do "means-to-an-end" living. Someone will say. "I am going to work for 40 years at a job or business that I hate so that one day I do what I want."

I'm sorry...but what?!

Who's going doing that? Well apparently, everybody does it because people are programmed to do that anyway. What a horrible life. What a horrible way to live.

Come on. Get with it.

This is fresh year, not 1905. You can do what you want to do in your eternal life I promise. Start doing it. There's no reason in saying, "I'm going to do something I hate so I can do something I love."

Forget that! That's bad for your optimal health and your beloved family. Do what you love to do and do it NOW! Don't wait for anything!

My friend; you may be unable to do it perfectly. You may be unable to do it in just the exact style you want to do it in, but it's a start.

Here are the three Master Class Pay Day® exercises for you to get started:

1. Make a list of five things you've always wanted to do but make up compelling reasons why you can't, shouldn't, or would never do. Not just five things you think would be "neat."

    I mean things that make you feel like, " Yeah, that'd be cool!" Things that make you smile and feel good when you imagine doing them.

2. Then write down those reasons you haven't done the things you've always said you wanted to do.

Write them down and then read them back to yourself ALOUD. Are those reasons and excuses that lead to a path of financial success?

Deep down, you know them to be wrong? Here's an example; if you decide to be a professional athlete but you're in your mid-life. It's not possible right? But perhaps maybe that's a good reason no to pursue that idea.

But if your reason for not starting a business because you fear how that will impact your family life and time. Well, that's just fear and outdated blueprints holding you back. Then for every reason "why you can't," come up with at least one reason why you can pursue what you want.

3. Pick three of those wants (or maybe all five) and start doing them! Start learning what you need to learn. Do some research.

Talk to people who are doing what you want and really good at it! Get some coachings or take a course.

One of the reasons to get rich is to be happy, but if on the journey to wealth you're unhappy, what's the use, my friend? Is it so you can roll over and die or have five years to enjoy it?

I went through that myself before. And that's why I know it's not the way to go. Start living as much of your dream life as you can right now. Let's start now with some smart secrets of budgeting below; are you excited? :)

Because setting an objective is the first intelligent key to a plan. Anything else you want to go through? Would you like correcting your revenue in bill transactions properly?

Would you like making a large buy or a large investment? You can form your plan to better represent your desires by setting a target.

Second, where your cash normally passes would you like to give notice. This applies to facts, large but frequent shopping (like food, education, etc.) and everyday acquisitions of various kinds.

You will only be prepared to define which costs you can incur when listing where you understand your cash is generally going. Take into account what you can trim away on after you have recognized these periodic expenses.

How much more are you spending in the pleasant afternoon on your regular caffeine set? How much do you waste on your front gate supplies?

The sizeable is $1 or R 15 of these acquisitions amounts to over R3,600 a year! Install the amount you would pay for those small routine purchased in a small container instead of purchasing your expensive lattes or reading a newspaper in print. You'll be amazed at how much of your elderly plan you're efficiently storing.

NEVER BE BROKE AGAIN

We do not want anything more than being willing to handle our cash effectively. However, the cash we want to handle is often difficult won cash. There is a bill here. A well-functioning plan should assist you see where your cash goes, get more utility out of each penny and save some additional for use in the lifetime.

Indebtedness is a devastating process alone. You talk about ongoing transactions, not to mention enormous inflation. In order to prevent charging extraneous early charges, you can charge the minimum on all your loans.

No matter which money excess you have, you can choose to attach to your largest transfers. In this manner, you focus on receiving the highest debt, which costs you the highest loan prices. If you do that gradually, how much you get out of your enormous loans is going to be astonished.

NEVER BE BROKE AGAIN

The final stage is to estimate the quantity you receive the quantity you invest. You can create use of desktop cash management programs or create your own database pages. Create a system to keep track of your monthly budgeting progress. This will help you.

Start using this new secrets of keeping to the family budget

Financial issues generally occur because the budget lacks adequate capacity or because the budget proposal does not comply. It is still essential to monitor your property and obligations, your earnings and expenditures, regardless of what amount of revenue you can earn.

It's high living costs of culture today, wherever you are, have created budgeting a concern for households. Nothing is more essential in today's inflationary globe than understanding how to budget the low revenue you get.

NEVER BE BROKE AGAIN

That's funny, but a guy who's earning thousands will have the same issues with the individual earning hundreds. More often than not, distinct types of individuals have budgetary issues at distinct rates of revenue. Many who have been able to make a profit generally do not stick to that plan.

A project relates to a financial plan that takes into account incoming and unused monetary assets. A healthy deficit should not just imply an income-expenditure equilibrium or capital. It often implies lower costs and a pension bonus.

When you gain a thousand bucks a month, you should chart all the costs you need to incur during the month, such as compensation for your home, meals but also travel. This assumes, of course, that you have already resolved your tax liability. Your savings remain after you deduct your total revenue costs.

When the need arises, what you do about your savings will change later. You can opt for saving in a money box or position your savings in a bank with a lowest interest rate, but you and intruders at least have cash securely.

You can obtain the facilities of a financial advisor with greater economies, who can provide you with higher returns on capital.

Here are suggestions to ensure that you stay within your household plan:

1. Keep your notebook on a week or monthly timetable, in which you can log your revenue and expenses report.

2. At one moment, buy your food. To do the same, record and buy everything you would need for your destination span at once. Occasionally, if you purchase by a couple, there are discounts. You can use it.

   3. If you don't have to purchase needed products, avoid moving to the store and stores.

NEVER BE BROKE AGAIN

You will not shop unnecessarily and will avoid distracting you from your plan.

4. Think about something times before you purchase. You understand that this is not really a requirement, but a caprice.

Here's the real reason why you can budget like Mom

She utilizes neither complex equations nor card tricks, but easy cleverness and good sense. In budgeting and learning, peek through the mysteries of moms. Modeling of roles is a useful manner to promote attitudes towards cash in particular.

It's actually the most ladies ' land. Besides their traditional part, women have an instinct and foresight for what could occur in the future, as the one who accounts for household funds.

However, how do moms extend their expenditure?

1.   She understands where all the cash is going. Typically, apart from accommodation, wellness coverage, meals, and apparel, it comes to childcare. Cutting costs on her kids is impossible for her.

2.   She explores all of her childcare alternatives. She investigates all elements such as security, wellness, and schooling before she chooses.

3.   She speaks to local childcare experts to know more and operates out plans for a mating moment with children with her boss.

   4. It's twice the undertaking for operating moms. They bring the charge of the home and the kids and operate simultaneously. Practical methods to achieve both functions are incorporated.

Carrying specialist clothing rather than fashionable clothing.

• By combining fundamental colors, it remains sophisticated but easy.

NEVER BE BROKE AGAIN

- It charges a heavy quantity of dry washing, so she donates on dresses for washing and wearing.

- Demeanor the items down.

- She has a bunch of do-it-yourself practices in her private wardrobes, such as washing places and ironing wrinkles.

    5. Mothers always store to maintain a record of their expenditure and spending with a roster in her pocket. She ensures she's not going beyond that. She also has no moment at the mall to check out appealing things.

Bridget (My Wife) surprised me with 10 tips to avoid shopping shortages

It is a tough job to save money. There is much to consider, especially how you can plan your cash, that would be accurate for what it should be used if you could not exceed surplus remaining money.

Money management is truly a throat pain. Your distribution of petrol charges, air facts, telephone charges, and so on are just a few of the many considerations regarding the wise use of your money. There's no issue regarding food.

As the most significant obligation of all households, we prioritize how to spend our funds and cut the cash invested without sacrificing the distribution of meals. We primarily purchase food supplies.

This would be of assistance if you name down items you have to purchase together with their prices (if possible) so as to ensure that the spending plan allocated for groceries is precise or there is a scarcity. If this is the case, you can reduce your lists or consider a better substitute.

In addition, here is some advice to prevent grocery shortages.

- Chart items to be discovered in the refrigerator at all times. Specific instances include tea, coffee, milk, sugar, soya sauce, ginger, spice, onion, cinnamon. Such products are needed, so they are always purchased.

- Sufficiently prepare your daily dinners in advance. You would prevent excessive expenditure or the lack of certain components. It would not only clarify your concerns but save your moment as well.

- Do not purchase a marked item; rather, choose an item that has the same value as that costly item. Without investing more, you'll get the same advantage.

Purchase multi-purpose products. Mayonnaise is a nice illustration of that. You can use it as a split plate or create a salad. In a manner, both of you could appreciate dining without investing too much.

- Purchase cheaper food reductions. List the ingredients that will not affect the reductions. You will not at least sacrifice the flavor of the meat and you will also have the opportunity to purchase a bigger amount.

- Cash payment. You may be encouraged to purchase useless items. You won't be able to exceed your ticket threshold.

- At the same moment, try being inventive and innovative. Remnants could be precooked to make your hunger feel attractive again.

- Take sweets every time you're traveling. This might help alleviate your appetite across the manner and the chance to shop in a small shop; at least be relieved if it is unfeasible.

- Hold a roster of commodity rates that you always purchase. At least you are aware of how much you spend with these products and you can make only a tiny quantity on goods you want to purchase.

- Shop just 1-2 times a month. This reduces the moment invested in a food shop while minimizing the likelihood of over-expenses.

Do not save your money without this

Official statistics indicate that the earnings of every bank account holder are declining considerably and that a rise in the monthly withdrawals has shown that individuals have little cash to invest on before their next card hits.

With shops, innovation accessibility, and increasing health care costs, borrowing, and increasing inflation, it has become very hard for one to invest less and save cash for potential usage.

This reality demonstrates a comparative rise in the quantity of expenditure in the marketing of distinct products by personal organizations.

Although these details and many tentations are common in the true globe, you can avoid hype by many methods and help you build up and construct your own private and distinctive practice of earning a few bucks from your fundamental wage.

- Obsessive Buying–7 out of 10 individuals love to buy a private product they like in a shop at first sight, given enough cash.

In a virtual sociological research, if they take their private bankcards with them, individuals who initially intended on window shopping finished up purchasing private items.

Limit your expenses to some bucks when you do windows-shopping and attempt to list them as soon as you plan to purchase them. Just buy the items in the store you need to leave those that do not meet an immediate requirement.

- Saving money–It is important to maintain an organized, efficient and yet reasonable money management technique along with your pursuit of saving for retirement. Budgeting eliminates buying temptations that would tend to build up during malling and help you save money along the process due to preformed lists of items you need to buy.

- Similarity of price performance–The World Wide Web offers a great way to provide a price list for certain items that you schedule on buying.

If you buy bulk and plan your malling business at one location, this is great for you. Doing so will give you a better idea if the usual shop where you usually get all your daily family needs gives you a competitive price for particular products.

NEVER BE BROKE AGAIN

- At home, you can prepare all conveniences–lunch, snacks and main meals at home. You can make all this from home and get some intestinal services by replacing soda with water if you are serious about saving money. This isn't just good for your wallet, it also does much for your wellbeing.

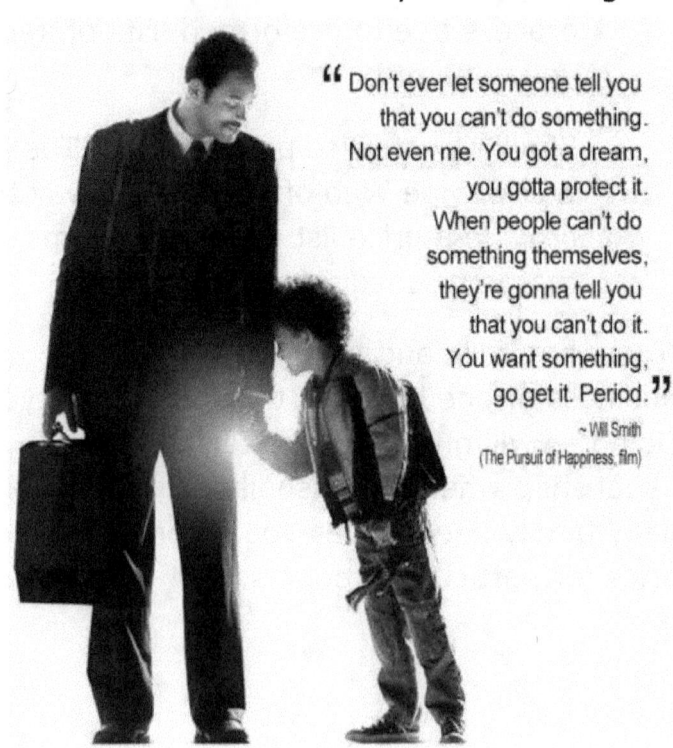

" Don't ever let someone tell you that you can't do something. Not even me. You got a dream, you gotta protect it. When people can't do something themselves, they're gonna tell you that you can't do it. You want something, go get it. Period."

~ Will Smith
(The Pursuit of Happiness, film)

NEVER BE BROKE AGAIN

11 BONUS! CHAPTER

To people who want to create wealth but can't get started

#1.WALLET FILE

2 Critical Questions Every Money Saver Must Answer

Remember, a problem that can be solved by writing a cheque is not a problem anymore. And in my experience, 90% of all problems can be solved with a cheque.

The number one reason most people don't get what they want is that they don't know what they want.

Please read this with me: Clarity leads to power. And power is what? Power is the ability to do or act as simple as that.

Unfortunately, most people commit themselves to financial freedom without realistic clear set of goals.

NEVER BE BROKE AGAIN

It's like playing golf all over the yards and you never find a hole. Is that make sense? I bet you said; NO!

So what's your realistic clear set of goals for your journey to financial freedom? Listen closely here; most people make a lot of money, save some, retire and spend the money they saved.

However, there's a very big problem with this thinking.

Do you see the problem with this?

If you spend all the money, you save, you will be killing your precious investment piggy bank. Here is the golden secret: The essence of cracking your financial freedom journey code is choice. And when it comes to money choice leads to financial freedom.

Let us lay the cards on the table and examine them. To change lines, just like driving a car, you signal attention. Right?

When I was still young, I used to hear the expression: "Live within your means." I think nowadays, we need to correct this expression by changing "within" to "below."

Sometimes, we have the uncontrollable habit of buying things we don't actually need, especially when items are "on-sale."

I hate to say this but probably some products are excessively produced on purpose, to be put up "on sale" if not completely sold while on a regularly priced.

Here it is the secret:

It's a free advertisement at it's best. The product makers don't lose money anyway. On the contrary, they make more money.

Here's the tip of an iceberg:

Buy things "on-sale", only if you would intend selling them for profit. Keeping a reasonable quantity is justifiable. Be prudent. This is one habit that you need to improve.

If you are making enough or more enough, keep in mind that it is not how much you make that can make you financially free. It's how much you spend and how much you keep.

With the cash you keep; books are some of the best investments. They keep you skillful. They open up new horizons which can lead to creating wealth.

The same thing is true with seminars, workshops, coachings, tapes and other media related to acquiring financial knowledge.

Will you be able to use more cash? Who couldn't, naturally?

If you're flooded with charges and expenditures or just looking to save some additional money for a pleasant household holiday, there are basically only two options:

1. Make more cash? OR

2. Reduce your fees?

It's simpler said than finishing to make more cash. Many individuals get just a rise in wages, which only includes inflation and higher personal costs. Increase medical costs, and many people have less money in their wage packet!

You may receive recognition and gain more, but it may take a while. But also how safe are you feeling at a job in this day and age of huge cutbacks?

You may discover a fresh job paying more, or you can get a part-time job. However bring from those who've been working extra-time employment to get stressful bits, and you have to bid farewell to many of your spare time.

It is less probable that lowering your charges will trigger significant conflict in your career. It's not as hard as you might believe to cut your costs and find methods to save cash. Everything you need is believed in creativity and outlook.

NEVER BE BROKE AGAIN

Take a glance at your cash, sit down and being honestly on it. You will be probably amazed. Some individuals every day, often without even being aware, cast cash down the river. Have I really gotten the greatest prize for my shirt? Ask yourself those topics?

Can I pay less in my garage for this fresh vehicle?

Can I leave when I am prepared or do I have to continue operating till I die?

Your responses were, hopefully, yeah, no and yeah. Otherwise, you likely missed a chance to save cash.

It is a skill that not everyone learns to learn how to save cash and attain economic safety. It's not something that's studied in colleges indeed. Below are some suggestions to get you to think about how you can improve your economic condition.

Make a choice of what you care about. Want to resign soon? Buy a larger house?

Are you on a fantasy holiday? Built these targets and remember them whenever you invest.

Consider whether or not it's worth putting off your dream before you leave R100 on a cup of coffee.

Consider how you can reduce your charges: can you pay down your loan at a reduced interest rate if you own your own house? While lending rates are beginning to shrink away, they are still at record levels. By paying down you could save hundreds of bucks.

What's your credit card like? You can move your equilibrium to a reduced rate card if you pay a heavy interest rate and save large cash.

Several cards now give an opening bid of 0 points for one year or more! Convert the balance and reward the most when the 0 percent offer expires. Only make sure you don't have a large equilibrium running once more.

NEVER BE BROKE AGAIN

Take a look at your credit score. It relies so much on your credit score. How would you understand if there is an issue or an error? You should always keep a close watch on it. If you realize something is wrong, get it fixed right away.

#2. WALLET FILE

The 30-Seconds money saving exercise you can be proud of

If you've ever sensed something is holding you back from being able to have more money or if you feel like there could be an invisible glass ceiling holding you back from greater level of your financial freedom journey, then I've decided to do something awesome to support you even more with the information below:

There is an easy practice to save cash that everyone must do in their life at least once. Eventually, it's one of the greatest places to save cash, because it's not about trying to save money, but about finding and having what you really want. You may refuse to attempt it so easy. Simply attempt it. Here it is: a record of all that you've invested in, presently spend on or could spend on.

Also, don't read and think about a couple of stuff. Consider taking the moment to write down everything. If necessary, check your bank reports to understand and include everything.

Check the list now and consider each item thoroughly. Start taking the most moment on the major problems–previous, current and future opportunities. Since your vacation share is worth twice what you earned, lives R20,000 a year in expenditure, and is scarcely used, you need to know from that– not to reward yourself, but to have a happier life.

When you seriously think about a couple of times, you're using that Medicinal Car and the cost, it can be R3,000 per day of usage. That's all right if it's meaningful to you, but you'd really appreciate R2,000 more in restaurants. But you may be able to lease a motor home at a lower general price, saving up cash for other significant objectives.

See, it's not really about sacrifice spending wisely. We are most conscious of the rubbing tightwads of childhood, managing money, and then doing nothing about it.

The conclusion should be to focus on saving cash in one section of your lives to create your entire lives happier.

Think you noticed that you spend R100 a month on magazine subscriptions that you don't write, or you almost never drive on bikes? You withdraw or give your bike subscriptions and what have you wasted? Is this an enormous thing? Instead, what is R100 going to get you?

- Invest it for 10 years, and take a second vacation with R15,000.

- Use this to settle once a year for a week off the job, to enjoy with the children.

- Trade it, to get an additional R700 per month through your elderly years.

- Purchase six nice good reads per year in a fascinating way.
- Create fruit divides for your household every month.
- Offer R2,000 a year to a valuable purpose.

If used intelligently, R100 per month can do a lot. Assume what else can you do if R3,000 per month has stopped being wasted. And that is why exploring what you want and what you don't want is so essential. It is one of the smartest ways of saving cash.

"Shoot for the moon even if you miss you'll land among the stars"
Les Brown

#3. WALLET FILE

Ask me anything about how to save money when travelling

Therefore please pay close attention. Before you ask me anything about how to save money when traveling. I have a very important financial life lesson to share with you today. Are you ready?

Hence, this is not a message to take it lightly.

Here it is...

Financial freedom success is a habit. It's not what you do once in a while, it's every day.

I always dazzle with my audience by saying these words; if I spent a day with you on my seminar or workshop. I would be telling you how successful you would end up. Some people often find this as a somewhat pompous statement, but I don't mean it to be that way.

The point here is that the secret to your financial freedom lies in your daily schedule. What do I mean by that? What you do consistently you become.

If you want to change your financial life, change your daily schedule. It is pretty obvious good decisions create a better destiny.

The point is, nobody says that good decisions are always simple, but they are necessary for financial success and progress. You start to winning the financial freedom journey by making better decisions. Now let's focus on how to save money when traveling.

It may be an excellent experience to travel, particularly abroad. It can, in addition, be a costly one for many individuals, meaning you need to understand how to save on costs.

Traveling is the supreme way to reinvigorate their zest for existence for many individuals. On the one side, you get away from the continuous disruptions in everyday life at a job and home.

But on the other hand, even if it's in your nation, you can see a whole distinct manner of staying in another place. Of course, the only issue with flying is that it can bring an edged sword on your account.

It is not so difficult to save cash when moving. The first part that needs to be remembered is that almost everything is up for negotiation. If not, for example, the price of trips, there are often timing problems, which can save money. There are hundreds of advice, but you may not know a few.

It is an excellent place to save cash to travel in a team. Travel companies like associations because they constitute a secured field of cash. When you can spin a band of 15 individuals for a journey, you will be offered free of charge by restaurants, cruising operators and others. Not the whole community, you alone.

It can feel like an odd approach, but it can function if you're angry about a place. You just give a directed visit to the place and promotional activities.

The price of your journey is nearly nothing and the rest of your income may be canceled. Make sure your advisor runs it, of course.

It should be understood that the cost of each space is negotiable when it goes to hotel reservations. A hotel assigns four, five and even ten different rates to each type of room they have.

They naturally want to get the most, but they give all kinds of offers in quiet moments to draw reservations. It's simplest way to use this is via internet hotel reservation locations. As these locations transfer huge amounts of reservations, the smallest or nearest price rates are generally achieved. You only have to match, point and click rates.

When you're flying by flight somewhere, you will eventually need personal transport. The cost of car hire at airlines is usually comparable to the city alternatives. The best way to get a deal is through your frequent flyer miles if you need to hire at the airport.

Tariffs maybe half the amount advertised at the desks. When you do not have frequent flyer points, attempt booking for the different rental businesses through internet locations. An amount of them will serve bonuses that can actually add up to large savings.

Baby steps can create all the distinction to save cash on journeys. Pursue the above guidance, and your bank balance should show fewer drain.

#4. WALLET FILE

What happens when you are saving money through investing in real estate?

The fact is, the fastest and easiest way to create wealth is to learn exactly how rich people (people who have already crossed that bridge), who are masters of money. The goal here is to simply model their inner and outer strategies.

It just makes sense; if you take the exact same actions and have the exact same mindset, chances are good that you will get the exact same results.

Are you ready to create wealth habit by modeling and associating with only rich, positive and successful people?

Choose one person whose successful and/or career path you'd model or follow. Then, each day, spend 5 to 10 minutes researching this person's career path and/or journey to success.

Use their story for inspiration, for learning specific success strategies, and most importantly, copying their mind-set.

When finished, announce these words out loud, "If they can do it, I can do it." This will act as your trigger and a signal to your mind that you associate and model with successful people only.

Join a high-end club, such as tennis, health, business, or golf etc. (or my goodness I like golf). Mingle with successful people in a productive environment. Or if there's no way, you can afford to join a high-end club, have a coffee or tea in the classiest hotel in your city.

Get comfortable in this atmosphere and observe the patrons, noticing they're no different than you.

Today, the rated-out idea in the world of financial systems is how to save cash by spending in immovable assets. Worldwide investors are attempting finding creative methods and methods to create cash quickly.

Some prolific writers also authored several novels on how to increase cash by spending on immovable solutions. In contrast to other equity instruments, immobilization provides you the liberty to readily to recover the cash.

Most seniors now rely strongly on long-term asset planning to guarantee a secure and hassle-free pensions career, according to recent press accounts. You can buy and hold the finest choice if you want to generate riches.

To save cash via equity, the business situation and subsequent risk management must be assessed appropriately. However, you can increase your revenue at a much quicker pace than just storing cash with smart maneuvers and correct business strategies.

In this regard, media accounts concentrating on international business strategies are universal. Very few shareholders for the first time do not know how to use a loan as an equity money-enhancing instrument.

So the investing tips outlined below may come handy in case you are contemplating with the idea of saving money by making investments.

- Reduce your tax revenue — actual property investments enable different tax cuts and thus reduce your tax revenue. It has become a popular mode of saving money these days.

- Wealth management–The proper management of your assets also helps to save cash and create wealth a long way.

It implies that if you take control of your estate in a timely manner, you will be saved from spending additional money when your house's situation is way out of hand.

NEVER BE BROKE AGAIN

It's more like a time-saving patch of nine. A further variable that contributes to your bank account is that your estate's fair value is maintained at a lucrative pace by managing it well ahead of time.

- Increasing money flow by increasing monthly mortgage–A further simple and common way to generate wealth is to raise your monthly rent for your leased buildings, which could result in thousands of rands being produced each year.

You should always consult the word of an current deed to prevent creating poor business decisions. You should first attempt to know from the failures of other people. To create the right choices, you can go through the property investment association and partnership records database.

Putting money in property development is no longer an imagination for you to create and save cash.

Recently, news accounts concentrating on banks providing business consulting facilities in global economies reach the news and are also being adopted around the world.

Saving is simply about handling your assets instead of asking where it came. Then next time you think about saving cash, consider the possibilities that you have described above to invest cash and become richer.

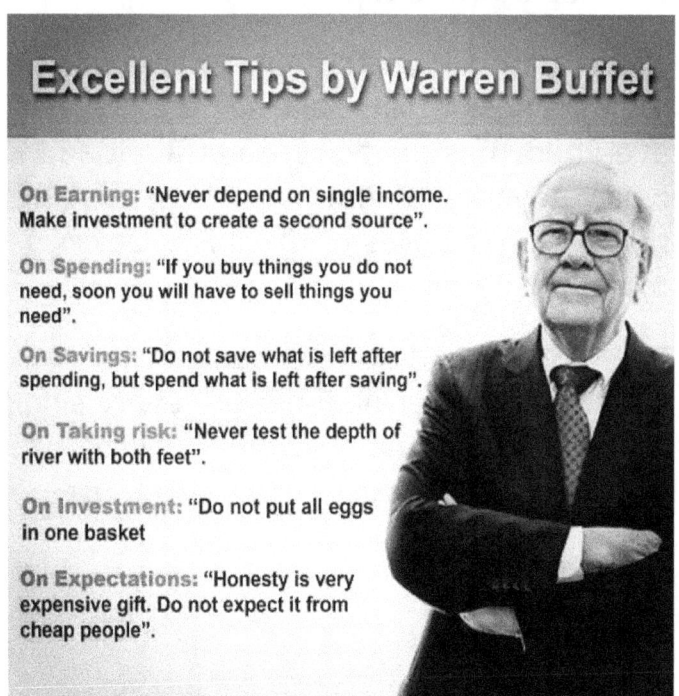

NEVER BE BROKE AGAIN

#5. WALLET FILE

Own this 10 killer tips on how to save money like a miser

So many people are in the pursuit of financial freedom, and I want to share with you today why they never get there.

It boiled down to this:

There are four simple things that eliminate their chance of financial freedom, however, everybody has the ability to attain it and I believe everyone right now who is reading this book has a Master Class Pay Day® mindset by now.

The problem is that most people are ambushing their true inner gift every single day by allowing the below four wealth killers to dictate their lives.

1. Time- Where you will be in 20 years from now will also be an accumulation of time depending on what you do between now and then, so I urge you to stop wasting time and ignite the Master Class Pay Day® strategies within you.

2. Procrastination- It is not a growth strategy, ask yourself when was the last time you procrastinated? How has it served you? How many opportunities have you let slide because of it?

3. Incompletion- There is a huge number of people who are never able to finish off what they have started.

4. Fear- How many times have you heard that fear is the choke-hold of success and wealth? Fear is an illusion we create in our minds, it doesn't even exist. In this book allow me to show you how you can conquer your fears and allow Master Class Pay Day® NEVER BE BROKE AGAIN to shine on you.

Extra cash is what it does, as per a modern definition. And, they're saying, the truth is like a band of rubber. Extend it and it can do miracles. There is none of that if we can really make cash to do whatever we want.

Providing ten fast suggestions for saving cash is almost like a first-aid strategy to a very complex issue that almost all of us might face.

To guarantee massive savings, it is essential to understand how to effectively handle cash. It is the first issue that should be addressed whether we can save some of what we have to invest or waste on a product or product at all.

Next, in the event of big investments, identifying and correlating the precious product or service with need or willingness is the first step for a potential customer. For instance, by lending it for a set length of a moment, it is easier to first check its utility.

You can purchase it if you're happy and persuaded of its existence and believe you really need it. However, in order to save cash, you need to discover the best seller as a reasonable customer in aspects of relative value, performance & notoriety on the industry.

For reduced cost products, you have to store at the smallest rates, maintaining an eye on the performance element as well. If you follow the example of buying clothes, for instance, the best sale is off-season reduced-price sales, where you can get nice clothes at low rates.

For investments, such as the share market, obey the golden rule of purchasing fragile stocks when an asset's cost is down and exchange it at a premium. The gain thus gained for constant products can be spent in the financial market.

Modern Internet has given the greatest possibilities for the greatest cost to store strongly before you simply leave the cash. One is spoiled for decisions, particularly for healthcare, credit equipment, and money management.

Decent rate and depreciation assessment run a lengthy manner in earning even hundreds of bucks a year.

Shifting the scheme can save you expensive bucks for facilities such as telephone, insurance, etc. if you merely have an understanding of the finest current scheme.

Trying to make a monthly bill to purchase vital products and regulate the number of luxurious products can generate substantial gains.

It is important to replace expensive nights and lavish outings with decent wholesale amusement excursions.

Financially and emotionally, proper meal scheduling and food habits lead to better living. Keep safe and on health charges, you can save. It also stops the meat from being lost by having an adequate meal scheme.

Paying the fees within the owing periods offers valuable money, because in this situation, as you have to settle, it is easier to budget in order to prevent fines.

Unless you are an employer, you should support versatile taskforce duties to make each work in a workplace compliant. It will assist reduce costs for staff and assist them to finish a job in a timely manner if somebody is away.

Apparently there are several other methods to save cash and live frugal, tension-free lives. It's often said that borrowed cash is gained cash. Bear it in mind and be pleased.

#6. WALLET FILE

The buzz 3 words everybody is talking about...Money Is King

I don't want to scare you, but...

Have you ever thought about what could happen if you never reach your financial goals?

Do you know somebody that is struggling financially, emotionally or physically in their life right now? No matter what they seem to do they just can't get out of their own way. And here's why?

From my experience in working with people all over the world, the key factor that gets in the way of people isn't getting what they want in life is the negative chatter of the little voice. I consider it a public enemy.

The little voice is the voice in people's heads that is always telling them why they're " not good enough","not smart enough", "too young...Or old" and that sabotage their efforts to get what they really want from life.

What would it mean to you if you could help your family, friends or associates to address the things that may be holding them back from leading a happy and fulfilling life? Now, I may be a little biased, but quite frankly, I believe it is one of the greatest gifts one human being can give another, and that is the gift of growth and hope. In this book; Master Class Pay Day® I want to help you so that you can be able to help them too.

If you're still struggling to make your financial dreams come true or making really slow and painful progress toward achieving them, then you really need to read this chapter till the end.

NEVER BE BROKE AGAIN

By the way here's an example story of Roger Bannister: "For a thousand-years human tried to run a mile in under four minutes and for 9 years ago the record stood at 04:01 (four minutes and one second). Public opinion was that it couldn't be done, until in 1954 when Roger Bannister did "the impossible." Five years later a further 20 people had run a sub-four-minute mile."What does this telling you about believing something is possible?

Don't waste any time, and energy worrying about your future, instead spend your time wisely by tuning into what feels right and doing something about it.

If you are ready to start making your financial goals your reality and to find your true purpose in life, then make sure you pay close attention below to the buzz three words everybody is talking about…Money Is King

You can alter your lives indefinitely if you comprehend and obey money King's fundamental concept.

Your existence is less socially exhausting and you will take your first significant move towards economic ease of opinion.

Money is a King, but it can be hard to comprehend, but money is a simple rule. That's the secret to reducing pain in your economic lives. Much says how to handle our funds and none of them appears to tackle the main source of our economic issues.

The greatest challenge is that we're living in a disposable world and we don't regard the importance of money for all practical reasons.

You will begin on the path to economic tranquillity if you pursue this easy but distinct concept that money is King. Below are two fundamental recommendations on how to pursue the Money King concept:

Make sure that you distribute sufficient cash when you are paid to pay your rent/hypothecary, services and any other specified costs you might have.

NEVER BE BROKE AGAIN

The certain money that is remaining should be withdrawn for meals, clothing, donations, recreation, petrol etc from your bank account. The easiest method for you to manage this money would be to split, allocate, and place a certain amount of money in envelopes such as the envelopes discovered in the structure budget keeper for each variable cost.

Today keep in mind the one way you can spend this money. There will be no expenditure until your next salary once you've used all of your money. It's hard! Are credit/debit cards not available? You have to be joking! How do I get back to my original paycheck without my credit/debit cards? We claim that smoking cigarettes are difficult to give up, I believe it may be even difficult to adhere to money concept!

Keeping money is King and handling your savings. You may find the best locations for the purchase of petrol, begin with your orders rationally and bring tea from the house in the afternoon instead of purchasing it each day.

You need to discover many fresh methods to handle your money and it will be hardest for you in the first few months. Before your next paycheck, you may not even come out of money, but you'll keep to the money concept and finally discover economic calm.

Before your next payday, it will become simpler to handle your money after several weeks and you will be amazed to discover additional money accessible. What are you going to do with the additional money? Some claim you placed the remaining money in a bank or settle one of your bills for a little cash. I tell you to bring it in tea and let it pile up and have a big celebration!

You will be on your manner to creating a private / household fund if you can follow this concept. Let the Process from budget keeper demonstrate you the path to economic harmony.

NEVER BE BROKE AGAIN

ABOUT THE AUTHOR

Who is Titus Maduwa?

He is something of a force of nature in the world of a personal, finance and business development.
Master Class Pay Day® founder, Pioneer of World Class Trading Secrets® program & Creator of Millionaire Pillars™ Book Writing Academy.

Titus Maduwa is highly connected with many elite South Africans, World Global International Speakers & Entrepreneurs and know what it takes to create success in today's economy.

NEVER BE BROKE AGAIN

Conclusion

At one of his very limited series of coaching, seminars or workshops: He will guide you through the steps you need to take to create your own meaningful life master plan tailored to you.

You'll also learn what you need to know about:

- How to earn, save and grow your money through multiple streams of income.
- How to prepare your mindset.
- How to set goals and be a goal achiever.
- How to write your first book in 90 days.

He has been one of the most highly regarded experts in his field for over a decade.

NEVER BE BROKE AGAIN

NEVER BE BROKE AGAIN